This Planner Belongs to:

_____

Table Of Contents

Special Notes

Personal Information

Special Notes

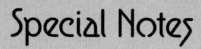

Personal Information

FULL NAME		
Christian Name	Middle Name	Surname

CURRENT ADDRESS			
Street & No	City	State	Country

IDENTIFICATION		
Drivers License No.	Social Security No.	Passport No.
Birth Certificate No.	Marriage License No.	Tax No.

MARITAL STATUS			
Married ☐	Single ☐	Divorced ☐	Widow/Widower ☐
Spouse Name	Telephone	Cell	Email

EMPLOYMENT			
Name of Employer	Address	Telephone	Email

Personal & Need To Know Notes

Emergency Contacts

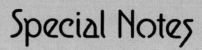

Special Notes

Emergency Contact Info

Contact	
Relationship	
Phone/Email	

Contact	
Relationship	
Phone/Email	

Contact	
Relationship	
Phone/Email	

Contact	
Relationship	
Phone/Email	

Contact	
Relationship	
Phone/Email	

Contact	
Relationship	
Phone/Email	

Emergency Contact Info

Contact	
Relationship	
Phone/Email	

Contact	
Relationship	
Phone/Email	

Contact	
Relationship	
Phone/Email	

Contact	
Relationship	
Phone/Email	

Contact	
Relationship	
Phone/Email	

Contact	
Relationship	
Phone/Email	

Family Contacts

Special Notes

Family Contact Info

Contact	
Relationship	
Phone/Email	

Contact	
Relationship	
Phone/Email	

Contact	
Relationship	
Phone/Email	

Contact	
Relationship	
Phone/Email	

Contact	
Relationship	
Phone/Email	

Contact	
Relationship	
Phone/Email	

Family Contact Info

Contact	
Relationship	
Phone/Email	

Contact	
Relationship	
Phone/Email	

Contact	
Relationship	
Phone/Email	

Contact	
Relationship	
Phone/Email	

Contact	
Relationship	
Phone/Email	

Contact	
Relationship	
Phone/Email	

Family Contact Info

Contact	
Relationship	
Phone/Email	

Contact	
Relationship	
Phone/Email	

Contact	
Relationship	
Phone/Email	

Contact	
Relationship	
Phone/Email	

Contact	
Relationship	
Phone/Email	

Contact	
Relationship	
Phone/Email	

Family Notes

Friend Contacts

Special Notes

Friends Contact Info

Name	Phone	Email	Address

Friends Contact Info

Name	Phone	Email	Address

Friends Contact Info

Name	Phone	Email	Address

Friends Contact Info

Name	Phone	Email	Address

Pets

Pet Info

Name

Type

Gender   ☐ Male   ☐ Female

Breed

Notes

Pet Photo

Pet Info

Name

Type

Gender

☐ Male   ☐ Female

Breed

Notes

Pet Photo

Veterinarian Record

Date	Reason	Results

Beneficiary & Legal Information

Special Notes

Beneficiary & Legal Contacts

Item	Contact Name & Number	Location
Solicitor/Attorney		
Power Of Attorney		
Accountant		
Beneficiary		

Special Notes

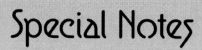

Important Documents

Important Documents

Item	Location
Will	
Birth Certificate	
Wedding Certificate	
Citizenship	
Financial Planner	
Medical Records	
Passport	
Advanced Directive	
Safe Deposit Box	
Tax File Number	
Business Number	
Business Records	

Important Documents

Item	Location

Thoughts & Doodles

DATE: _____

Insurance Policies

Insurance Policies

Type	Policy No.	Company	Contact
Life			
House			
Contents			
Auto			
Other			
Travel			
Medical			

Finances

Special Notes

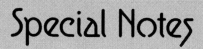

Bank Accounts

Type	Bank	Routing No.	Account No.

Investments

Type	Details	Account No.

Credit/Debit Cards

Type	Bank	Account No.	Monthly Payment

Loans

Type	Bank	Account No.	Monthly Payment

Car Details

Type	Account No	Company	Payments
Auto Repayments			
Vehicle Registration			
Third Party Insurance			
Comprehensive Insurance			
Roadside Assistance			
Repairs & Maintenance			

Household Accounts

Type	Account No	Company	Contact
Mortgage			
Rent			
Electricity			
Gas			
Telephone			
Cell			
Medical Insurance			
Cable TV			
Internet			

Household Accounts

Type	Account No	Company	Contact

Other Accounts

Type	Account No	Company	Contact

Subscriptions

Special Notes

Online Subscriptions

Type	Account No	Company	Monthly Payments

Online Subscriptions

Type	Account No	Company	Monthly Payments

Online Subscriptions

Type	Account No	Company	Monthly Payments

Other Subscriptions

Type	Account No	Company	Monthly Payments

Social Accounts

Special Notes

Online Social Accounts

Type	Login	Password	URL

Online Social Accounts

Type	Login	Password	URL

Passwords

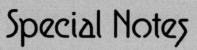

Special Notes

Password Tracker

	Site		Password
1.			
2.			
3.			
4.			
5.			
6.			
7.			
8.			
9.			
10.			
11.			
12.			
13.			
14.			

Password Tracker

	Site		Password
1.			
2.			
3.			
4.			
5.			
6.			
7.			
8.			
9.			
10.			
11.			
12.			
13.			
14.			

Password Tracker

	Site		Password
1.			
2.			
3.			
4.			
5.			
6.			
7.			
8.			
9.			
10.			
11.			
12.			
13.			
14.			

Password Tracker

	Site		Password
1.			
2.			
3.			
4.			
5.			
6.			
7.			
8.			
9.			
10.			
11.			
12.			
13.			
14.			

Where Things Are

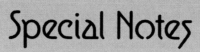

Special Notes

Where To Find Documents

Item	Location	Completed/Notes
House Deeds		
Life Insurance Papers		
Drivers License		
Bank Books		
Auto Insurance		
Funeral Insurance		
House Insurance		
Contents Insurance		
Social Security Card		
Medical Card		
Birth Certificate		
Wedding Certificate		
Citizenship		
Passport		

Where To Find Documents

Item	Location	Completed/Notes

Where To Find Documents

Item	Location	Completed/Notes

Where To Find Documents

Item	Location	Completed/Notes

What Do They Look Like?

Item

Item

Item

Notes

_____

_____

_____

_____

_____

_____

Where To Find Things

Item	Location	Completed/Notes
House Keys		
Car Keys		
Medications		

What Do They Look Like?

Item

Item

Item

Notes

_____

_____

_____

_____

_____

_____

Where To Find Things

Item	Location	Completed/Notes

What Do They Look Like?

Item

Item

Item

Notes

Where To Find Things

Item	Location	Completed/Notes

What Do They Look Like?

Item

Item

Item

Notes

_____

_____

_____

_____

_____

_____

What To Do With Things

What Do They Look Like?

Item

Item

Item

Notes

_____

_____

_____

_____

_____

_____

Distribution of Items

Item	Recipient	Completed/Notes

What Do They Look Like?

Item

Item

Item

Notes

What Do They Look Like?

Item

Item

Item

Notes

_____

_____

_____

_____

_____

_____

Distribution of Items

Item	Recipient	Completed/Notes

What Do They Look Like?

Item

Item

Item

Notes

Distribution of Items

Item	Recipient	Completed/Notes

Checklist

- ☐ _____
- ☐ _____
- ☐ _____
- ☐ _____
- ☐ _____
- ☐ _____
- ☐ _____

- ☐ _____
- ☐ _____
- ☐ _____
- ☐ _____
- ☐ _____
- ☐ _____
- ☐ _____

Other Things To Do

Topic	Activity	Reason/Outcome

Other Things To Do

Topic	Activity	Reason/Outcome

Health Care Information & Directives

Medical Contacts

Type	Name	Contact No.	Location
General Practitioner			
Dentist			
Optician			
Specialist			
Surgeon			
Oncologist			

If I Can't Make Decisions

Choices For My Last Days

Where I want to stay

_____

_____

Company or Alone

_____

_____

Visitors I would Like

_____

_____

_____

_____

Music /Songs to Listen To

_____

_____

_____

Funeral Plans

Special Notes

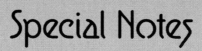

Funeral Arrangements

My Preferences:

How

Where

Music

Funeral Home

Funeral Arrangements

Who To Invite

_____

_____

_____

_____

_____

_____

_____

_____

_____

_____

_____

_____

_____

_____

_____

_____

Ceremony of Remembrance

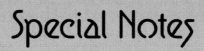

Special Notes

Ceremony Of Remembrance

Ceremony Of Remembrance

Photo's To Include

Memories are made like this

Photo's To Include

Memories are made like this

Photo's To Include

Photo's To Include

My Life & Memories

Favorite Photo's

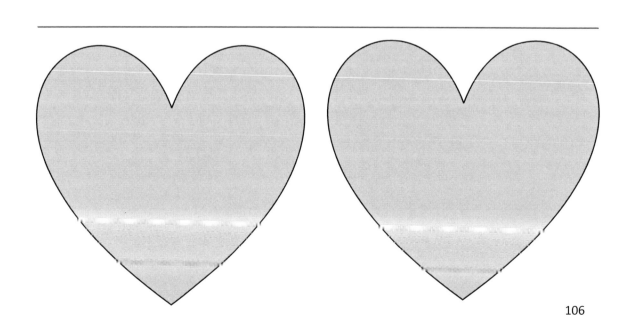

My Special Wishes

My Special Wishes

Messages For My Family

_____

_____

_____

_____

_____

_____

_____

_____

_____

_____

_____

_____

_____

_____

Messages For My Family

_____

_____

_____

_____

_____

_____

_____

_____

_____

_____

_____

_____

_____

Messages For My Family

_____
_____
_____
_____
_____
_____
_____
_____
_____
_____
_____
_____
_____

PHOTO'S

Memories are made like this

Favorite Memories

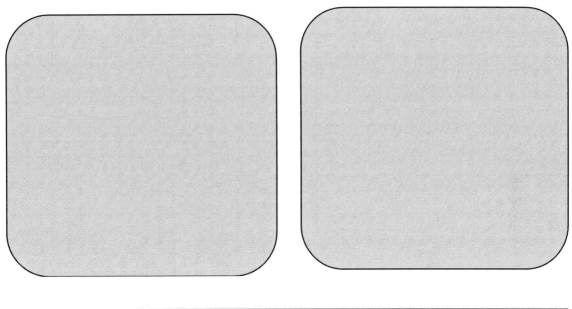

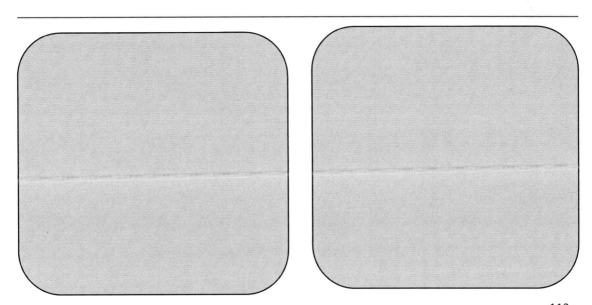

Favorite Memories

Date	Memory

Achievements

Date	Achievements

Achievements

Date	Achievements

Thought's & Reflections

_____
_____
_____
_____
_____
_____
_____
_____
_____
_____
_____
_____

For Myself

ALWAYS BELIEVE IN the impossible

HAPPINESS IS BEING A Grandparent

For My Family

Don't Cry Because It's Over Smile Because It Happened.

Hopes For My Family

_____
_____
_____

Reflections on Life

In Conclusion... .

Just a few last observations about my life ... _____

_____

_____

_____

_____

_____

_____

_____

_____

_____

_____

_____

Life is a Journey Enjoy The Ride

Disclaimer

Made in the USA
Monee, IL
17 May 2022